To: _____

From: _____

THANK YOU
for Your SERVICE

Published by Sellers Publishing, Inc.

161 John Roberts Road, South Portland, ME 04106

Visit us at www.sellerspublishing.com • E-mail: rsp@rsvp.com

 Like Us on Facebook

Copyright © 2014 Sellers Publishing, Inc.

Images © Shutterstock

All rights reserved.

Compiled by Mary L. Baldwin

ISBN-13: 978-1-4162-4539-1

Printed and bound in China.

10 9 8 7 6 5 4 3 2 1

THANK YOU
for Your SERVICE

A Tribute to the Brave Men & Women
Who Serve Our Country

Dear soldier,
Thank you for answering
the call to serve.

—GERARD WAY

Courage.

Kindness.

Friendship.

Character.

These are the qualities

that define us as human beings. . . .

—R. J. PALACIO

Courage is what preserves our liberty, safety, life, and our homes and parents, our country and children.

—TITUS PLAUTUS

Courage is found
in unlikely places.

—J. R. R. TOLKIEN

It is from numberless
diverse acts of courage
and belief that human
history is shaped.

—ROBERT F. KENNEDY

Courage and perseverance have a magical talisman, before which difficulties disappear and obstacles vanish into air.

—JOHN QUINCY ADAMS

With courage and character, American soldiers continue to put themselves on the line to defend our freedom. . . .

—CONGRESSMAN DAN LIPINSKI

Freedom lies
in being bold.

—JACK FROST

Leadership is a potent combination of strategy and character.

—GENERAL NORMAN SCHWARZKOPF

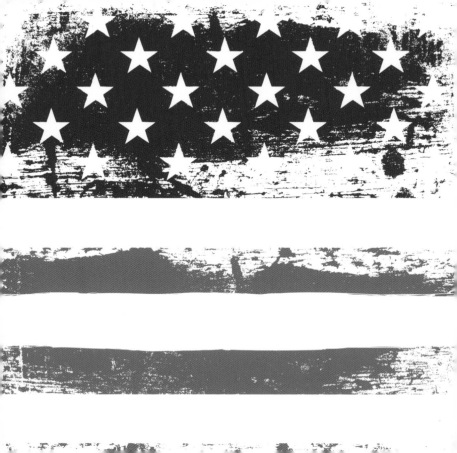

This nation will remain

the land of the free

only so long as it is

the home of the brave.

—ELMER DAVIS

Bravery is believing in yourself, and that thing, nobody can teach you.

—EL CORDOBES

**Bravery never
goes out of fashion.**

—WILLIAM MAKEPEACE THACKERAY

Without the brave efforts of all the soldiers, sailors, airmen, and marines and their families, this Nation . . . would not stand so boldly, shine so brightly and live so freely.

—LANE EVANS

It is a
proud privilege
to be a soldier.

— GENERAL GEORGE S. PATTON, JR.

There is a certain enthusiasm in liberty, that makes human nature rise above itself, in acts of bravery and heroism.

—ALEXANDER HAMILTON

Where liberty dwells,
there is my country.

—BENJAMIN FRANKLIN

Heroes are made
by the paths they choose,
not the powers
they are graced with.

—BRODI ASHTON

Heroes are ordinary people who make themselves extraordinary.

—GERARD WAY

How important it is for us
to recognize and celebrate
our heroes and she-roes!

—MAYA ANGELOU

We will never forget the many sacrifices you have made each and every day.

—UNKNOWN

Honor to the
soldier and sailor
everywhere,
who bravely bears
his country's cause.

—ABRAHAM LINCOLN

Liberty

means

responsibility.

—GEORGE BERNARD SHAW

Life without liberty is like a body without spirit.

—KHALIL GIBRAN

It is not the strength
of the body that counts,
but the strength
of the spirit.

—J. R. R. TOLKIEN

The power of noble deeds
is to be preserved and passed
on to the future.

—GENERAL JOSHUA CHAMBERLAIN

We often take for granted the very things that most deserve our gratitude.

—CYNTHIA OZICK

All the great things are simple . . .

freedom, justice,

honor, mercy,

duty, hope.

—WINSTON CHURCHILL

No one is more cherished
in this world than you
who lightens the burden
of another.

—UNKNOWN

Our freedom is brought to us courtesy of the outstanding men and women who serve and have served this country with honor, dedication, pride, and sacrifice!

—UNKNOWN

We need to thank all our troops,

particularly those for whom

we can never express enough

gratitude for they have given

their lives so that

all of us may be free. . . .

—VIRGIL GOODE